Oregon Coast Memories

Bandon Beach, sunset

Oregon Coast Memories

Rod Barbee

The Countryman Press
Woodstock, Vermont

Book design and composition by Susan McClellan, Irish Hill Design

Published by The Countryman Press, P.O. Box 748, Woodstock, VT 05091
Distributed by W. W. Norton & Company, Inc., 500 Fifth Avenue, New York, NY 10110
Printed in China

10 9 8 7 6 5 4 3 2 1

Oregon Coast Memories
978-0-88150-988-5

▲ Cannon Beach, from
 Ecola State Park

Introduction

VACATION—WHAT A WONDERFUL WORD! Eating out, driving around, doing what you want when you want—why does anyone ever go home? Ok, there is that work thing, but life is too short to work all the time. Isn't it time to start planning your next trip, your next fun adventure? Where to this time?

How do your pictures turn out on vacation trips? Do you get some good shots? All nicely sorted and labeled and presented, are they? You must get up early and stay out all day with camera in hand, chasing the best light. Do you wait for those perfect moments, when the action is just right and everything looks perfect?

Well, of course not. You're on vacation! You have better things to do than wake up before dawn and wait around with your camera all day. You have fun all the time and you take pictures when you can. But don't worry! That's why there are professional photographers: somebody has to be out there taking pictures when everyone else is having a good time!

This book is for you, the fun people out there; consider it your personal photo album of the area. Hundreds of miles were driven, hours and hours were spent, and thousands of images were taken over many months to get the best of the best pictures for this book. We might not have taken *every* beautiful picture possible out there, but we believe we got most of them.

If, when looking through this book, you find that a favorite place was left out, I do apologize, but that just means it will stay hidden and private and "yours" a little while longer. If, on the other hand, you'd like to share your photos of favorite spots in this area, I have just the thing for you: Go to www.tcpmemorybooks.com and post your pictures of favorite places that should be included. Think of it as your own online second edition.

I'm thinking Washington, DC, or California's Wine Country or Vail, Colorado, would be good places to go next on vacation. Ready? See you there!

David Middleton, *series editor*

▶ Girl dancing
   around a sand castle,
   Cannon Beach

◀ Cape Blanco
Lighthouse, sunset

Oregon Coast Memories

EACH YEAR HUNDREDS OF THOUSANDS OF VISITORS vacation along the Oregon coast. They come in summer, they come in winter. They come to watch whales, surf, fish, bird-watch, golf, sample local wines, and stroll the beaches, exploring the tidepools. In fact, the coast is Oregon's number-one tourist destination. Hundreds of miles of sandy beaches and rugged coastlines, outstanding natural beauty, great local seafood, charming towns, and endless recreation opportunities draw visitors from all over the world.

Along the 363 miles of coastal Hwy 101, which stretches from Astoria in the north to the California border, are all kinds of attractions, among them many museums. There are logging and pioneer museums; lighthouse and maritime museums; antique auto, railroad, Native American, and WWII museums; and the world-class Oregon Coast Aquarium. Visitors will find myriad opportunities here to satisfy their intellectual curiosity.

Lighthouses might be the most popular sites on the Oregon coast. There are eleven lighthouses in all: two are private; seven are open to the public for daily tours; six are operational; and the rest were shut down or supplanted by automated warning beacons.

Oregon boasts one of the most extensive and well-maintained state park systems in the country. On the coast alone there are 86 parks, waysides, viewpoints, and recreation areas. Many of these provide direct access to beaches—all of them public. If you can get to a beach here, you can enjoy it.

And if you want to camp out, you'll find excellent accommodations in the state parks. Many parks offer campsites, many rent out yurts, and some even have comfy little cabins with kitchens and outdoor grills—happy campers love the Oregon coast.

No matter how you spend your time here, you'll enjoy yourself and you'll want to come back again. Next time maybe you'll visit a different part of the coast, or maybe you'll want to return to that quaint little town on the beach that you fell in love with; either way, chances are good you'll be back.

▶ Harris Beach, sunset

▲ Walking in front of a mural in Old Town Florence

◀ Fishing boat heading out at sunrise on a foggy
   morning, under Yaquina Bay Bridge

▲ Buoys, Yaquina Bay
   Harbor, Newport

▲ Crab pots

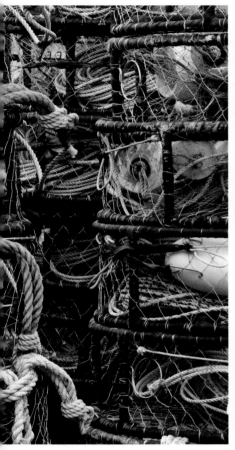

▲ Fishing nets, fishing
lines, and rope

◄ Wreck of the
Mary D. Hume on
a foggy morning,
Gold Beach

17

▲ Cook's Chasm, with Cape Perpetua in the background

▶ Low tide at Seal Rock State Park

Heceta Head Lighthouse, from viewpoint

◀ Morning on Crescent Beach with Cannon
Beach in the background, from Ecola
State Park

▲ Little girl enjoying her vacation,
Cape Lookout State Park

▲ Walking on the beach, Oceanside

◀ Surfers at Cape Kiwanda

▲ Statue of the Sea Hag and her husband outside
Gracie's Sea Hag restaurant, Depoe Bay

▶ Sculpture at Sea Lion Caves

◀ Sea nettles (*Chrysaora fuscescens*) in the Oregon Coast Aquarium, Newport

▶ Yaquina Bay Lighthouse, Yaquina Bay State Park, Newport

▲ Riding a quad on the sand
dunes, Oregon Dunes National
Recreation Area, near Florence

▲ Riding "quads" on the sand
dunes, Oregon Dunes
National Recreation Area

▲ 30th annual Seaside Beach Volleyball
Tournament, the country's largest
amateur beach-volleyball tournament

▲ Surfers at Cape Kiwanda

◀ Seagulls, Boiler Bay State Park

Cape Arago Lighthouse at sunset, near Coos Bay

▲ Fishing boats in
foggy harbor

▶ Annual sand-
sculpting contest,
Seaside

◀ Formal garden,
Shore Acres
State Park

▲ Formal garden, Shore Acres State Park

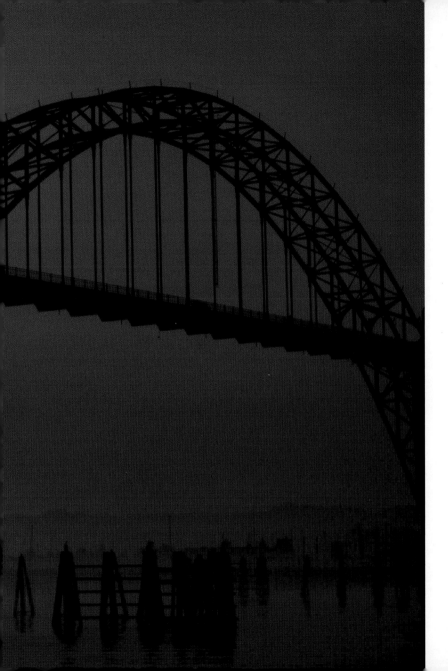

◀ Yaquina Bay Bridge

◀ Fishing buoys

⏶ Seal Rock State Park is a great place to
see tide-pool creatures and even the
occasional seal.

◀ Filleting albacore
tuna on the *Grace
Elizabeth* in Yaquina
Bay Harbor, Newport

▶ Tillamook Air
Museum

◀ View south from the
top of Cape Perpetua

▲ 30th annual Seaside
Beach Volleyball
Tournament

▲ Sea lions frequent the
docks in Old Town
Newport

▲ Returning to Depoe
Bay from a whale-
watching trip

◀ Redfish Rocks at sunset

◀ Hiking among the sea stacks of Bandon Beach, looking south from Face Rock Wayside

▲ Siuslaw River Bridge from Old Town Florence

▲ Tradewinds boat-tour and whale-watching ticket office, Depoe Bay

▶ Coast Guard exhibit at the Columbia River Maritime Museum, Astoria

▲ Depoe Bay Winery

▲ Visiting Ripley's
Believe It or Not in
Old Town Newport

▲ At Depoe Bay

◄ Tufted puffin at the Oregon Coast
Aquarium, Newport

▲ Cape Blanco Lighthouse in silhouette,
sunset

▶ Family enjoying the
  Passages of the Deep
  exhibit in the Oregon
  Coast Aquarium,
  Newport

◀ A boat is lifted
  out of the water
  at the Port Orford
  "harbor," where boats
  are stored on trailers

▲ Harbor seals at Strawberry
  Hill Wayside haul-out

◀ Sea Lion Caves

▶ Beneath the
Siuslaw River
Bridge in Old
Town Florence

◀ Haystack Rock and
visitors silhouetted
after sunset,
Cannon Beach

▲ Twilight in Newport Harbor

◀ Lightship *Columbia* and Coast Guard ALERT
vessel with Astoria Bridge in the background,
Columbia River Maritime Museum, Astoria

▶ Couple with dog,
Beverly Beach

▲ Cannon Beach on a cool August morning, with Tillamook Rock Lighthouse in the background

▲ Early morning on the Cedar Bend Golf Course, Gold Beach

▲ Flying kites at one of several
kite festivals along the coast

▶ Looking up into Cape
Blanco Lighthouse,
Cape Blanco State
Park, Port Orford

◀ Fresnel lens in Cape
Blanco Lighthouse,
Cape Blanco State
Park, Port Orford

◀ Inn at Otter Crest and
Devil's Punch Bowl
State Natural Area,
from Cape Foulweather

TRICERATOPS
Pronounced: try-SER-a-tops
Literally, "three horned face"
One of the plant-eating horned dinosaurs that
lived during the upper Cretaceous period, more
than 60 million years ago. He weighed from
6 to 8 tons, was 28 feet long and his
was fully one-third of his entire

▲ Prehistoric Gardens, on the coast

▶ Spouting whale sculpture, Depoe Bay

◀ Horseback riding on
Bandon Beach, with Face
Rock in the background

▲ Couple and crashing waves with
   Yachats in the background

◀ Sea lions on the rocks at Sea Lion Caves

▶ Samuel H. Boardman
State Park, looking
north from North
Island Viewpoint

▶ Low tide in
the morning,
Bandon Beach

◀ Wreck of the
Peter Iredale
at sunset, Fort
Stevens State Park

▲ "Le Cave": interior of
Depoe Bay Winery

▲ Carousel inside the
Seaside Carousel
Mall in Seaside

▲ Giant metal chicken
for sale at Flamingo Jim's
in Rockaway Beach

◀ Oregon Dunes National Recreation Area

▲ Contemplating another foggy morning on the coast, outside Jerry's Rogue Jets, Gold Beach

◀ Sculpture, Azalea Park,
Brookings

▶ Cape Meares Lighthouse

OREGON COAST MEMORIES

▲ Recumbent cyclist, Cannon Beach

▶ Sunset and sea stacks, Three Arch Rocks
National Wildlife Refuge

OREGON COAST MEMORIES

Late afternoon on the beach at
Cape Lookout State Park

▲ Fishing boats on a foggy morning, Charleston Harbor

▶ Yaquina Head Lighthouse, early morning, Yaquina
Head Outstanding Natural Area, Newport

▲ Lightship *Columbia* at the Columbia
River Maritime Museum, Astoria

◀ One of the many murals in Old Town
Newport

▲ Bicyclists, Cannon Beach

▲ Bonfires, Cannon Beach

▲ Haystack Rock and tourists at sunset,
Cannon Beach

▲ Tourists in the observation area at the Tillamook
Cheese Factory

◀ Production line at the Tillamook Cheese Factory

▲ A diver cleans the glass in the Passages of the Deep
display at the Oregon Coast Aquarium, Newport.

◀ Sea Lion Caves

◀ Fishing buoys piled
in the dock area of
Yaquina Bay Harbor

▶ Birdhouses at
Richard's gift store
in Rockaway Beach

▲ Street musician outside
  Lloyd's Old Town Tavern,
  Old Town Bandon

▲ Old Town Bandon

▲ Lotus Grotto Gifts,
Old Town Bandon

▲ Devil's Punch Bowl

◀ Astoria Column

▲ Friends on Agate Beach
at sunset